A Great Idea

The Jaws of Life®

by Toney Allman

NORWOOD HOUSE PRESS

Norwood House Press
P.O. Box 316598
Chicago, Illinois 60631

For information regarding Norwood House Press, please visit our website at:

www.norwoodhousepress.com or call 866-565-2900.

PHOTO CREDITS: Cover: Shutterstock; © Ashley Cooper/Alamy, 29, 33; Associated Press, 5, 10, 11, 13, 20, 24, 25, 35, 38-39, 42; Courtesy of Hurst Performance, 9, 14, 19, 21, 34; dmac/Alamy, 26-27; © Enigma/Alamy, 6; © Jack Sullivan/Alamy, 30; © M. Stock/Alamy, 25, 26-27, 40; Maury Aaseng, 16; NASA, 41; www.tes2training.com, 8

Paperback ISBN: 978-1-60357-080-0

The Library of Congress has cataloged the original hardcover edition with the following call number: 2008007041

This paperback edition was published in 2011.

Printed in Heshan City, Guangdong, China.
188P–082011.

Contents

Note: Words that are **bolded** in the text are defined in the glossary on page 44.

Chapter 1

Trapped in the Wreckage

Jeramy McMillen's car skidded on an icy Iowa road on February 3, 2001. It slammed into a telephone pole and flipped into the air. It ended up smashed and wrecked in someone's yard. McMillen was trapped inside the car. The door and dashboard were pushed against his body. A metal rod from the door was sticking through both his legs. **Rescuers** raced to the scene. With modern rescue tools, they freed him from the tangled mess of metal. McMillen's life and legs were saved.

Before the 1970s, McMillen's story might have ended differently. He might have died of his **injuries** before rescuers could free him from the car. In those days, victims of car crashes often could not be rescued quickly. Firefighters and rescue workers always worked as fast as they could. But sometimes cars were twisted and **mangled**. Car roofs caved in. Doors

Firefighters try to free a trapped passenger after a car crash.

were twisted shut. Whole car bodies were squeezed like **accordions**. Cars might rest upside down. In crashes involving several cars, one car could end up sitting on top of another. Rescuers could not get to the victims easily. Freeing a person trapped in a car was slow and difficult work.

Every Minute Counts

Rescuers did not always have many choices in how they went about this task. They could try to force open the car door. They could break a window or the windshield in hopes of reaching the victim. But that was risky. Flying glass could add to the victim's injuries.

One option was to call a tow truck company for help. Once they arrived on the scene, one truck would

Firefighters sit beside the body of a person who died in a crash.

?

Did You Know?

In 2006, 42,642 people died in motor **vehicle** crashes in the United States. That is an average of 117 people a day or one traffic accident-related death every 12 minutes.

hook up to one end of the car. The other would hook up to the other end of the car. Then the trucks would pull the car apart so that rescuers could reach the trapped victim. This system did not work very well. When a person is badly injured in a crash, every minute counts. The faster a victim gets treatment, the better chance

he or she has to **survive**. Many trapped victims have died before they could be rescued. It just took too long to get them out of their cars and off to the hospital.

Saws and Crowbars

Other times, rescuers used **crowbars** to pry apart the crushed metal. This was dangerous for the trapped victim. The force of prying on the metal could make a car move and tip. It could force other metal parts down onto the victim. Sometimes, trapped victims were injured even more as they were freed from their cars.

Rescuers also used big circular saws to get trapped people out. They used the saws to cut through the twisted metal. The power saws were dangerous, though. They made sparks as rescuers cut through metal.

These sparks could cause fires in cars that were leaking gasoline. The roar of the saws was bad for accident victims, too. It was scary to them and caused them great stress. Rescuers tried to reassure victims and keep them calm, but it was not easy.

Sparks caused by power saws could be dangerous during a rescue.

The noise of saws and jerking with crowbars made the problems worse. The flying sparks worried both victims and rescuers. Firefighters did the best they could. They tried to work slowly and carefully while not wasting any time. Sometimes it took hours to free trapped victims. And sometimes the victims died because they did not get to the hospital quickly enough.

Death at the Racetrack

What happened on the highways also happened on racetracks. Race car drivers today reach speeds of well

George Hurst

George Hurst was born in Pennsylvania in 1927. He dropped out of school after the eighth grade and joined the U.S. Navy when he was sixteen years old. After he left the military, he went home and got a job as an auto mechanic.

During the 1950s Hurst worked on cars and got involved in drag racing. He grew to love both. He did not have a formal education, but he was inventive and smart. Soon he started an auto repair shop of his own.

Then in 1958, Hurst set up a small company with his friend, Bill Campbell. They designed car parts for race cars. They hired Jack "Doc" Watson to help them. One of their early, famous inventions was the "Hurst shifter" for changing gears in a car. Drag racers replaced the regular shifters in their cars with Hurst shifters because they were powerful and tough. Hurst's company was very successful. His success in that company gave him the freedom and money to work on the Jaws of Life.

George Hurst (left) came up with the idea for the Jaws of Life after seeing slow rescue efforts at a racetrack.

A Dangerous Sport

The Indianapolis Motor Speedway is one of the most famous and popular racetracks in the world. Like all racetracks, it is a place of danger for drivers. Since the track was first opened in 1909, 41 racers have lost their lives at the track.

A race car hits the wall and bursts into flame during the Indianapolis 500. The driver suffered only broken bones.

over 200 miles (321km) per hour. Before the 1970s, drivers often hit speeds of more than 160 miles (257km) per hour. And at those speeds, crashes can be deadly.

British race car driver Mike Spence died in one such crash in 1968. During a practice lap at the Indianapolis Motor Speedway, Spence lost control of his car. The car slid 300 feet (91m) and then hit a concrete wall. It bounced another 390 feet (118m) along the wall, then skidded 290 feet (88m) more before it stopped in the middle of the track. Spence died of massive head injuries.

George Hurst, a businessman from Pennsylvania, was at the same

Fiery crashes like this one at the Indianapolis Motor Speedway were often fatal before the Jaws of Life.

track on a different day when another crash took place. In that crash, a driver was pinned in his car. The driver was injured and bleeding badly, but rescue workers could not get to him. The crew worked for more than an hour to rip a hole in the car and get the injured man out. By that time, it was too late. The driver was dead. Rescue workers had been unable to get to him in time to stop the bleeding.

Hurst and others in the crowd watched the **frantic** efforts to save the driver. Hurst thought later about what he had seen that day. He wondered how many other race car drivers had died because rescuers could not get to them in time. He worried that many others would suffer in the future.

An Inspired Idea

Hurst's company, Hurst Performance, was in the race car business. His company designed and built parts for race cars. So, designing and building a new rescue tool would not be hard. The tool that Hurst had in mind would act like a giant can opener. It would pry apart twisted,

Did You Know?

Motor vehicle crashes are the leading cause of death for 15-to-20-year olds in the United States. In 2006, 3,490 15-to-20-year-old drivers were killed and another 272,000 were injured in motor vehicle crashes.

crushed metal so that the victim inside could be freed. It would not be large. It had to fit on a fire truck or other rescue vehicle. It would not make sparks or increase the danger to the victim or res-

An Indy 500 race car slams into a wall. The driver survived.

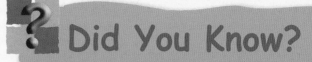
cuers. But it would be powerful. It would easily spread, push, or pull aside metal.

Back home in Warminster, Pennsylvania, Hurst talked with his team about his idea for the new rescue tool. The tool would snatch accident victims from the jaws of death. The tool would have jaws of its own that could crunch through metal. It would be a giant Jaws of Life.

Chapter 2

Hydraulic Rescue

The Hurst Performance team got to work right away. Engineer Jack Allen "Doc" Watson did the design. Another engineer, Mike Brick, was hired to develop and build the tool. Between them, Hurst, Watson, and Brick had a lot of knowledge and experience. They felt sure they could come up with a tool that would work.

The team talked over the problem and sketched their ideas. The tool had to be

Early versions of the Jaws of Life (above) showed promise but they weighed more than 500 pounds.

able to spread apart pieces of a wrecked car. It would act like a giant pair of steel scissors. But instead of the blades moving toward each other to cut, they would move away from each other to spread apart crushed metal. To be strong enough to do that, the tool would need engine power. The men decided to use a gasoline-powered engine. The engine would drive a **pump** that would work the scissor-like jaws. It would use **hydraulics** to create a powerful force.

Hydraulic Machines

A hydraulic machine uses a fluid to send force or pressure from one point to another. Vehicles such as bulldozers and backhoes are operated with hydraulics. So are the lifts for cars in mechanics' garages.

J.A.W.

During the design process, Jack Allen Watson drew up lots of ideas for the new rescue tool. He sent the drawings around the company for people to look over. He always signed his initials on the drawings: J.A.W. The design team started calling the new tool *Jaws*, after Watson's initials. That is how the tool got its name. When it was finished, it became Jaws of Life.

Hydraulic tools work with a fluid that pushes on a **piston** that is inside a tube or pipe. The piston is a solid **cylinder** attached to a rod. The rod is linked to a tool. A pump pushes fluid through the pipe and underneath the piston. The piston and rod are pushed upward by the fluid. This

How the Jaws of Life Works

1. Start the portable motor.
2. The motor turns on the pump, which pushes on the oil in the green hose.
3. The oil in the cylinder starts pushing the piston forward.
4. The piston's action gives force to the rod. A switch directs the oil to the red hose to force the piston backward.
5. The rod pushes or pulls the jaws open or closed to spread or cut.

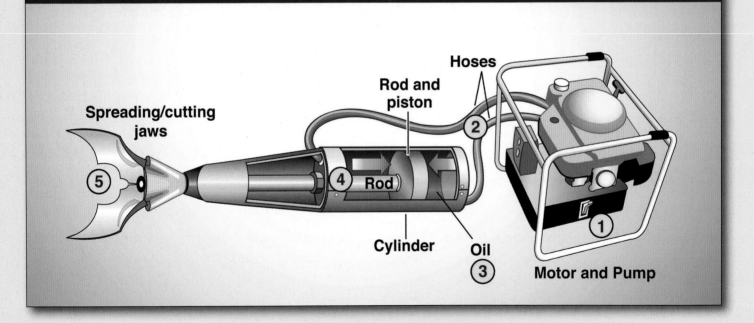

Spreading/cutting jaws

Hoses

Rod and piston

Rod

Cylinder

Oil

Motor and Pump

force is what operates the tool. If the tool is a giant pair of scissors, the scissors are forced open by the powerful push of the piston and rod.

The Right Fluid

In most cases, hydraulic tools run with oil. Pushing on the oil forces it through the hose, and the force of the piston's push increases when the oil hits its base. Pistons of different sizes can increase the force even more. A thin hose can drive oil under a wide, thick piston and create a very strong upward force.

Hurst's team did not want to use oil in their rescue tool. Oil easily catches fire. Heat or sparks from a car accident could cause a fire. They decided to use a **phosphate-ester** fluid instead. This fluid does the same job as oil but it is safer than oil at crash sites. It does not catch fire or conduct electricity.

The First Rescue Machine

Hurst's engineers built a hydraulic tool with a piston and rod inside. It had two hoses hooked to a pump and engine. The scissors blades were like jaws that opened and shut. When a rescuer started the engine, it provided the running power for the pump. The phosphate-ester fluid was pushed through one of two hoses to the piston. The fluid pushed on the base of the piston, driving it upward. The rod and piston were attached to a link at the bottom of the blades. The upward push of the rod forced the jaws to open. Flipping a switch on the handle of the jaws made one hose close and the other open. Now the fluid traveled through the other hose. The fluid forced the piston downward. This closed the jaws.

The constant opening and closing stretched metal apart in seconds. This was better than any power saw. It was fast. And it was safe. There were no sparks. And there were no dangerous bits of flying metal that sometimes resulted from sawing.

The tool worked just like Hurst wanted it to. And it was simple to use. But there was one big problem. It was big and it was heavy. It weighed 500 pounds (227kg). No one person could lift it or carry it. And the only way to get it to an accident was by attaching it to the frame of a rescue truck. Once at the scene, the only

Did You Know?

Emergency medical personnel refer to the 60 minutes immediately following a car accident as the "golden hour." Their goal is to get seriously injured victims to hospitals for treatment within one hour of when the accident took place. This is thought to give injured victims the best chance for recovery. Meeting this goal is more difficult when a victim is trapped in or under a car. This is why hydraulic rescue tools are such an important innovation.

George Hurst (third from the front) shows how his invention can lift a car.

Rescue workers in West Virginia practice using the Jaws of Life.

way to make it work was by using the truck's engine for power. Hurst and his team decided it had to be smaller.

Back to Work

Hurst, Watson, and Brick went back to work. Finally, they came up with a new design. This one weighed less than 100 pounds (45kg). It had its own engine and its own pump. These two parts together weighed 40 pounds (18kg). The jaws part of the tool weighed 55 pounds (25kg).

This meant that one person could lift and carry the rescue tool. That same person could open a 32-inch (81.3cm) hole in metal in less than one minute. The whole thing was small enough to fit into the trunk of

a car. The engine and pump that powered it had two long hoses that hooked to the tool itself. That meant that the engine could stay in the car trunk while only the jaws were

An early version of the Jaws of Life fits neatly into a box.

brought to the wrecked car. Hurst and his team named their new tool "Jaws of Life."

Everybody Wants One

Hurst Performance sold its first hydraulic rescue tool on December 28, 1971. It cost $3,775. Hurst had planned to sell his new tool to racetracks. But rescue squads and fire departments were his biggest customers. They knew right away that they could save lives with the new hydraulic tool.

The only problem: not many fire departments could afford one at the time. So people in towns and cities around the country held bake sales and fund-raisers. They raised money for local fire departments and rescue squads that wanted the new Jaws of Life. In the first year, the company sold 10,000 rescue tools. The world of car crashes and victim rescues was changed forever.

Chapter 3

Essential Rescue Equipment

Shannon was in a hurry. She was supposed to meet a friend to do some shopping on September 9, 2006 in Kirkland, New York. But she was running late. So she did not slow down even though it was raining hard and the road was wet.

Suddenly the wheels of Shannon's car skidded on a slick spot. The car slid off the road and ran down a steep **embankment**. It stopped only when it smashed into a large tree.

The tree's trunk split in two from the impact. The car also split in half. A splintered piece of trunk pierced the car just inches from Shannon's head. The half of the car where she was sitting was crushed. The steering wheel was smashed into her chest. Shannon was trapped in a space no larger than a toy box. The rest of the car was mangled and flattened.

The Jaws Save a Life

Shannon was alive, but she was badly injured. She could not move and struggled to breathe. Two men driving by in their van saw the wrecked car and called 911 for help. The wreck looked bad and they could not see the driver or any passengers.

Firefighters and rescue squads raced to the scene of the accident. They did not know if they would find anyone alive. They worked quickly but carefully. First they attached steel cables to the car to keep it from sliding down the hill.

Hydraulic rescue tools like the Jaws of Life are especially helpful in serious accidents such as this rollover.

With the Jaws of Life, rescuers can cut through metal and spread it wide.

Then they brought out fire extinguishers in case of fire. Next they pulled out their Jaws of Life. And then they got to work.

The firefighters cut into the car. Shannon was shivering and in shock, but she remembers hearing the sounds of metal tearing as the Jaws of Life started to work. Soon the rescuers had pried open a small hole. And that's when they spotted Shannon. She was alive but they could not reach her. She was pinned inside the twisted metal.

Using their hydraulic rescue tools, firefighters managed to pull the car's roof, side panels, windshield frame,

Rescue workers train using the Jaws so they know the best way to get injured victims out of a wreck.

dashboard, and trunk hood out of the way. At that point, a medic was able to reach Shannon. The medic gave her oxygen to help her breathe. But she was not yet free. Firefighters still had to cut away the metal that had trapped her legs.

Finally, an hour and a half after they had begun, Shannon was pulled gently from the car. She was raced to the hospital in an ambulance. She was bleeding badly and had broken bones, but she survived to tell her story. She knows that she lived because of the rescuers and their equipment.

In countries around the world, hydraulic rescue tools such as the Jaws of Life help to free trapped accident victims. Shannon's story is just one of many that take place each year. Hydraulic rescue tools have become essential equipment for rescuers ever since the invention of the Jaws of Life.

Modern Hydraulic Rescue Tools

In 1972, Hurst Performance was the only maker of Jaws of Life. Many companies now make hydraulic rescue tools. (Only Hurst tools bear the name "Jaws of Life," even though many people use the name to refer to all hydraulic rescue tools.)

Mike Brick, who worked with Hurst at the very beginning, started his own company in 1982. He is well known in the emergency rescue world. Some think of Hurst as the father of hydraulic rescue tools. Many others think of Brick as the

Stuck in a Box

Sometimes people get trapped in very odd places. In August 2007, a woman in England got trapped in a collections box for a local charity. She had dropped some of her used clothes through the slot of the box. But she changed her mind about the donation. To get the clothes back, she crawled headfirst into the slot. And that's when it happened. She got stuck—with only her ankles and feet sticking out. A passerby saw her feet and called the fire department. Firefighters had to cut her out with their Jaws of Life.

father of the *modern* rescue tool. Brick's company, Phoenix Rescue Tools, makes lightweight hydraulic rescue tools. For instance, one of his rescue tools weighs only 60 pounds (27kg).

Hurst's hydraulic rescue tools were the first of their kind, but now other companies offer their own versions, like this one by Lukas.

Hydraulic rescue tools are now so light that one person can hold them during a rescue.

Modern rescue tools do more than just pry apart metal. They push, pull, and cut metal, depending on the need. Brick's company produced the first hydraulic tools that could do all three things. Most other rescue tools can now do the same. Today's hydraulic rescue tools are actually a set of tools, and rescuers learn to use the whole system. The system includes cutters, spreaders, and rams.

Cutters, Spreaders, and Rams

Cutters cut through metal. They look like an overlapping pair of jaws that open and close to bite through vehicle metal in seconds. Cutters may be used, for example, to cut through the posts that attach to a car's roof. Then the roof can be lifted right off the car. Cutters can chomp through almost any part of a car's frame.

Spreaders are like a closed pair of thick-bladed scissors. The tips can be forced into the crack of a door and then opened. Firefighters call this operation a "door pop." When the spreaders open, they pop a door right off its hinges. Rescuers also can use the open spreaders for pulling power. One blade is attached with a chain to the frame of the car. The other blade is chained to the steering wheel.

When the open spreaders are closed, the steering wheel is dragged toward the frame. This can free a person who is trapped under the steering wheel.

Rams push apart hunks of crushed metal. A ram is just a heavy steel piston rod that can be extended with very great force. If a person is trapped under a crushed dashboard, the ram is set up underneath it. When the ram is turned on, the rod rams against the dashboard and pushes it off the victim. Rams can also be set up against the body of a car to brace it and keep it from rolling over.

Modern hydraulic rescue tools prove their value again and again. In the Northern California town of Oroville in December 2001, fire department rescue teams were sent to the scene of an early-morning

Modern hydraulic tools like this spreader by Lukas must be lightweight and be able to push, pull, lift, and spread metal.

The Green Cross Award

When rescuers save a trapped victim with Jaws of Life, they can report the rescue to Hurst. The company awards a Green Cross patch to every person involved in the rescue. The Green Cross is the symbol of first aid around the world. Thousands of people have received this honor and wear the Green Cross on their uniforms.

accident. A car had hit a power pole. Two people were trapped inside. Both were badly injured. Rescuers pulled the car away from the pole. And then, using their cutters and spreaders, freed the two injured people. Both were rushed to the hospital for life-saving surgery. And all of this took place in well under an hour.

Spreaders, cutters, and rams are the hydraulic rescue tools of today. Around the world, 35,000 rescue squads, fire departments, and police departments own these hydraulic tools. They are essential rescue equipment.

Chapter 4

More Great Ideas

Hydraulic tools helped rescue workers uncover survivors buried under the wreckage of the World Trade Center.

When New York's Twin Towers came crashing down in the attacks of September 11, 2001, the search for survivors began right away. Emergency personnel used hydraulic rescue tools to help find people buried in the **rubble**. With these tools, they raised heavy pieces of steel and concrete. They pried apart crushed, melted hunks of debris. Later, the Hurst company sent three truckloads of hydraulic rescue tools to help in the search for the dead.

Disaster Rescue

Hydraulic rescue tools are not just for car crashes anymore. They are used wherever someone is trapped. This can include buildings destroyed in accidents, war, terrorist attacks, or natural disasters such as earthquakes.

In 2005 in New Jersey, construction workers cut through a gas line by mistake. The accident set off an explosion. The explosion destroyed a large pet store. The building's roof and first floor caved into the basement. The walls were turned to rubble. Several injured people had to be rescued. One man lay trapped under a large air-conditioning unit that had fallen from the roof. Rescuers arriving on the scene with hydraulic tools cut the unit off the man. He was safely re-moved from the debris and rushed to the hospital.

Future Robots to the Rescue

Hydraulic rescue tools have shown their value over and over. They can mean the

Military Rescue

Hydraulic rescue tools have saved lives in many places, including in Iraq. In 2003, a helicopter carrying U.S. soldiers was shot down by enemy fire. The helicopter crashed, killing three soldiers. Two other soldiers were still alive but trapped when rescuers reached the crash site. Fortunately for the wounded soldiers, their rescuers had a Jaws of Life. The rescue squad pried the soldiers out of the mangled helicopter. The soldiers were then flown to a hospital. Both survived.

difference between life and death. In the future, hydraulic rescue tools may join with robots to save lives. In collapsed buildings, robots could crawl into small spaces that are too risky for people. The robots could carry a camera so that rescuers can see deep under the rubble. Knowing where to work can help rescuers reach trapped people much more quickly.

A company called Boz Robotics has gone a step further. It has put two great ideas, robots and hydraulic tools, together. It has built a rolling robot with hydraulic jaws. It is called the Boz robot. It is operated by remote control. The robot can grab a car with its powerful jaws. It can lift and drag the car away from buildings. This could be useful if a bomb were planted in the car. The robot can also be a

rescue tool. If needed, it can tear a car apart with its powerful force. It can rip off a locked heavy door to get inside a building, too.

The Boz robot cannot be used for helping trapped people yet. It might tear into a person by mistake. It still has to be improved so it will be safe for humans. But bomb squads today can use the robot to get inside a locked car and snatch out a bomb.

In 2007, the bomb squad of Columbus, Ohio, bought a Boz robot. It cost $300,000. Columbus firefighters believe it was worth the money. Now no firefighters will have to risk their lives to get at a bomb. Someday, a robot like this may also have a hydraulic rescue tool system.

Lighter and Stronger

The companies that make hydraulic rescue tools keep working to make them better. In 2006, one company invented a new cutter. It weighs only 46 pounds (21kg), but it has a stronger cutting force than any other cutter in

Boz, the remote-controlled hydraulic robot, can lift and drag a car and go to places too dangerous for people.

the world. It can bite through a 1.6-inch (4.1cm) steel bar in one snip. Another company has invented a new cutter, too. It has **serrated** blades and weighs just 38 pounds (17km). Because it is smaller than other cutters, it can fit into smaller spaces. It does not have the force of a regular cutter, but it can reach into tight spaces that larger rescue tools cannot reach.

New ideas are being developed all the time. One company has developed rescue airbags. They are like square rubber pillows. Firefighters can place these airbags under a vehicle and inflate them. The airbags can lift a whole car so that rescuers can free a person trapped underneath.

Companies have made other improvements too. It takes time to hook up hydraulic rescue tools to their motors. So, one company has found a way to avoid this problem. It has developed a hydraulic cutter called Lifeshear.

This cutter does not use a standard motor. It borrows technology from the National Aeronautics and Space Administration (NASA). After a space shuttle launches, it separates from the boosters that help lift it from the launch pad. Explosive bolts provide the power for that separation. Explosive bolts like these are built right into the Lifeshear tool. They fire over and over again to run the cutter. The cutter can be started up in 30 seconds. This is faster than tools run by a gasoline engine. But Lifeshear does not have quite as much power as tools connected to a regular engine.

The Space Shuttle inspired a new, faster cutting tool called Lifeshear.

Making Rescue Tools Safer

Hybrid cars present another problem for people working with hydraulic rescue tools. Hybrid cars use both a gasoline engine and an electric motor. The electric motor uses batteries for power. This electricity is a danger for rescuers. They could be **electrocuted** when they try to use hydraulic tools to get a victim out. "You don't want to go crushing . . . [hybrid cars] with hydraulic tools," one assistant fire chief in Pennsylvania told a news reporter. "It's enough to kill you from what they're telling us in training."

Hybrid car makers have added features to keep rescuers safe. New hydraulic rescue

Special new hydraulic tools were designed for use with hybrid cars to prevent rescuers from being electrocuted.

tools have also been developed for use on hybrid cars. The tools are made so that they can be used around electricity. Rescuers can use them safely, even when they cut into battery parts and cables. Trapped victims can be freed, but rescuers are protected from danger during the rescue.

To Save Every Life

The makers of hydraulic rescue tools never stop trying to improve them. They believe that no one should die in an accident because rescuers cannot get him or her. Jaws of Life was one great idea that

Virtual Practice

Freeing trapped victims with hydraulic rescue tools takes practice. Today, rescuers can practice their techniques on a computer. A new software program lets users choose from 20,000 different virtual vehicles. The user clicks on a vehicle and then removes the parts one at a time. That way, rescuers know how to safely remove any part of any car to get to a trapped victim.

inspired more great ideas—whole sets of rescue tools to snatch people from the jaws of death.

Glossary

accordion: A musical instrument that folds in and out in order to make sounds.

crowbars: Steel bars that can be used as levers.

cylinder: A solid or hollow object with straight sides and circular ends.

electrocuted: Killed by an electric shock.

embankment: A hill or slope off the edge of a road.

frantic: Hurried and excited.

hydraulics: In engineering, the science of using moving fluids to operate machines.

injuries: Damages done to someone's body.

mangled: Damaged too badly to be fixed.

phosphate-ester fluid: A thick liquid that is often used to run hydraulic machines because it does not catch fire.

piston: A solid cylinder inside a larger hollow cylinder that moves up and down because of pressure from a fluid.

pump: A device that forces liquid, air, or gas into or out of something.

rescuers: People whose job it is to save people from accidents.

rubble: Smashed-up pieces.

serrated: Notched or saw-toothed.

survive: To live through something difficult.

vehicle: A car or truck.

Books

Marshall Brain, *Marshall Brain's MORE How Stuff Works*. Hoboken, NJ: Wiley, 2002. This large book explains the workings of many kinds of everyday technology. One section explains both hydraulic machines and Jaws of Life.

Allan B. Cobb, *Extreme Careers: First Responders*. New York: Rosen, 2007. Readers are introduced to emergency medical technicians, firefighters, and rescue experts who risk their lives to save others. Daring and exciting rescues are described, as well as the training needed for these careers.

Janet Piehl, *Indy Race Cars*. Minneapolis: Lerner, 2007. Readers can explore the world of Indy cars, the Indianapolis Motor Speedway, the drivers who race, and the dangers they face.

Web Sites

HHFD Heavy Rescue "Jaws of Life" (www.hasbrouck-heights.com). This site from New Jersey's Hasbrouck Heights Fire Department includes step-by-step pictures and explanations of a training exercise in setting up and using Jaws of Life. Visitors can click on a series of links to see real cars being dismantled with hydraulic rescue tools.

How the Jaws of Life Work (http:// auto. howstuffworks.com/jaws-life.htm). This detailed article explains how the hydraulic rescue tools work and provides a link to learn about how hydraulic machines work. Animated drawings of pistons help explain the tools.

Hurst Jaws of Life (www.jawsoflife. com). This is the home page of Hurst Jaws of Life. The company is no longer run by George Hurst. It has a new owner but it still makes hydraulic rescue tools. Visitors can explore the site, see the latest equipment, and learn the history of the company.

Phoenix Rescue Equipment (www. phoenixrescue.com). The company started by Mike Brick still produces hydraulic rescue tools. Visitors can click the links to watch the tools in action.